this or that?

monkey

OR

ape?

Susan Kralovansky

Consulting Editor, Diane Craig, M.A./Reading Specialist

Super Sandcastle

An Imprint of Abdo Publishing
www.abdopublishing.com

visit us at www.abdopublishing.com

Published by Abdo Publishing, a division of ABDO, PO Box 398166, Minneapolis, Minnesota 55439. Copyright © 2015 by Abdo Consulting Group, Inc. International copyrights reserved in all countries. No part of this book may be reproduced in any form without written permission from the publisher. Super SandCastle™ is a trademark and logo of Abdo Publishing.

Printed in the United States of America, North Mankato, Minnesota
062014
092014

 THIS BOOK CONTAINS
RECYCLED MATERIALS

Editor: Liz Salzmann

Content Developer: Nancy Tuminelly

Cover and Interior Design and Production: Mighty Media, Inc.

Photo Credits: Kelly Doudna, Shutterstock

Library of Congress Cataloging-in-Publication Data

Kralovansky, Susan Holt, author.

 Monkey or ape? / Susan Kralovansky ; consulting editor, Diane Craig, M.A., reading specialist.

   pages cm. -- (This or that?)

 Audience: 004-010.

 ISBN 978-1-62403-287-5

1. Monkeys--Juvenile literature. 2. Apes--Juvenile literature. I. Craig, Diane, editor. II. Title.

 QL737.P9

 599.8--dc23

                     2013041833

xSuper SandCastle™ books are created by a team of professional educators, reading specialists, and content developers around five essential components—phonemic awareness, phonics, vocabulary, text comprehension, and fluency—to assist young readers as they develop reading skills and strategies and increase their general knowledge. All books are written, reviewed, and leveled for guided reading, early reading intervention, and Accelerated Reader® programs for use in shared, guided, and independent reading and writing activities to support a balanced approach to literacy instruction.

contents

monkey or ape?

Is it a monkey? Or is it an ape? Can you tell the difference?

Apes and monkeys are both **primates**. But apes are bigger than most monkeys. Gorillas are the largest apes.

Monkeys are usually smaller than apes.

a tale of tails

Most monkeys have tails.
Apes do not have tails.

Orangutans, bonobos, gorillas, and chimpanzees are apes. They are called great apes. Gibbons are called lesser apes. They are smaller than great apes.

get moving

Apes have many ways of moving around. Sometimes apes walk on their feet and the **knuckles** of their hands. Sometimes apes use their arms to swing between tree branches. Sometimes apes walk on their **hind** legs like humans.

Monkeys move around in many of the same ways apes do. They often walk on their hands and feet. But they do not walk on the **knuckles** of their hands like apes. A few monkeys can walk on their **hind** legs.

Most monkeys are arboreal. That means they live in trees. Many arboreal monkeys live in rain forests.

that's smart

Apes have large brains.
They are some of the
smartest animals on earth.

Chimpanzees are good at making tools. Many use stones to **crack** open nuts.

Monkeys are less **intelligent** than great apes. But they are still smart. Some monkeys rub their fur with special plants that **repel insects**.

Some monkeys can be trained to help people. Capuchin monkeys have been taught to help disabled people. They do things such as open **drawers** and turn pages in books.

make some noise!

Gibbons are loud! Siamang gibbons have big
pouches on their throats. These pouches
let them make loud booming **noises**.

Many monkeys are **noisy** too. The loudest is the howler monkey. Their calls can be heard from miles away.

that's handy

Apes have four fingers and a thumb on each hand. Apes also have four fingers and a thumb on each of their feet.

Monkeys have four fingers on both their hands and their feet. Some have thumbs on their hands and some don't. But they all have thumbs on their feet.

at a glance

monkey ————————— ape

smaller in size ——————— larger in size

has a tail ——————————— no tail

walks on flat hands ——— walks on **knuckles** of hands

lives in trees ——————— lives on the ground

thumbs on feet but not ——— thumbs on both hands and feet
always on hands

monkeying around craft

use paint and a marker to make a swinging monkey!

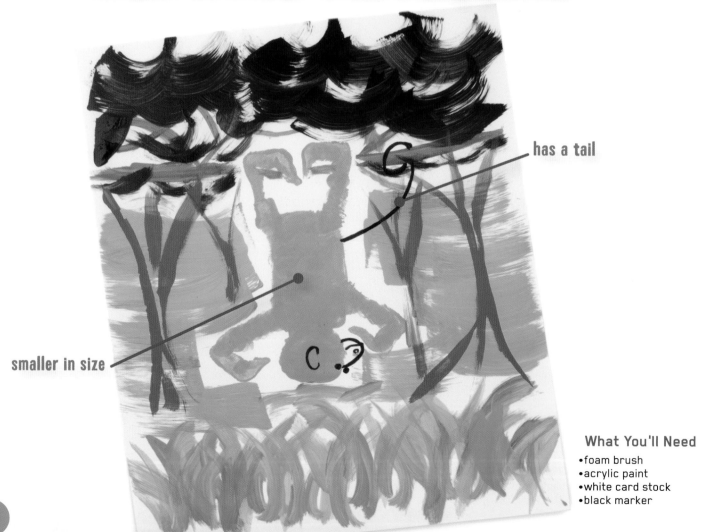

has a tail

smaller in size

What You'll Need
- foam brush
- acrylic paint
- white card stock
- black marker

1 Paint the edge of your hand. Make a fist. Press your fist onto the card stock. Turn the card stock around. Press your fist onto it again to make an oval.

2 Dip your finger in paint. Use it to fill in the oval. This is your monkey's body. Dip your thumb in paint. Press it to the card stock twice to make the head. Wash the paint off your hand.

3 Paint the edge of your hand again. Curl just your fingers. Keep your **palm** straight. Press your hand onto the card stock to make one arm. Turn the card stock around. Press your hand onto the card stock to make the opposite leg. Paint the edge of your other hand. Make the other arm and leg the same way. Wash the paint off your hands.

4 Paint a **background** for your monkey. Paint trees, grass, and sky. Let the paint dry.

5 Draw your monkey's face and ears with a marker. Draw the tail wrapping around a branch.

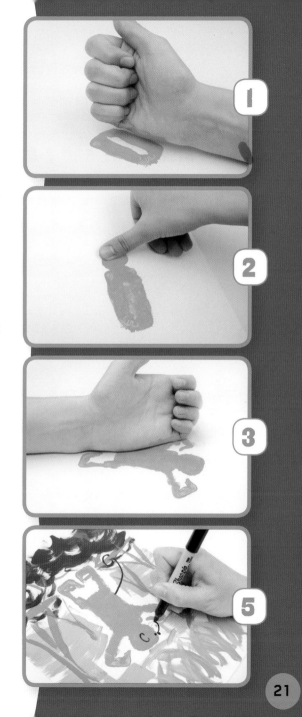

let's go ape craft

use paint and a marker to make a standing ape!

larger in size

no tail

What You'll Need
- white card stock
- black marker
- acrylic paint
- foam brush

1. Draw a circle on the card stock. This is your ape's head. Draw the face and ears. Draw a large oval below the head. This is the body.

2. Paint the edge of your hand. Make a loose fist. Press your fist onto the card stock to make one arm. Turn the card stock around. Press your hand onto the card stock to make the opposite leg. Paint the edge of your other hand. Make the other arm and leg the same way. Wash the paint off your hands.

3. Dip your thumb in paint. Use it to fill in the body. Dip your finger in paint. Paint the upper part of the face. Wash the paint off your hand. Dip your finger in a different color of paint. Paint the lower part of the face. Wash the paint off your hand. Let the paint dry.

4. Re-draw any marker lines that got painted over.

5. Paint a **background** for your ape. Paint trees, grass, water, and sky. Let the paint dry.

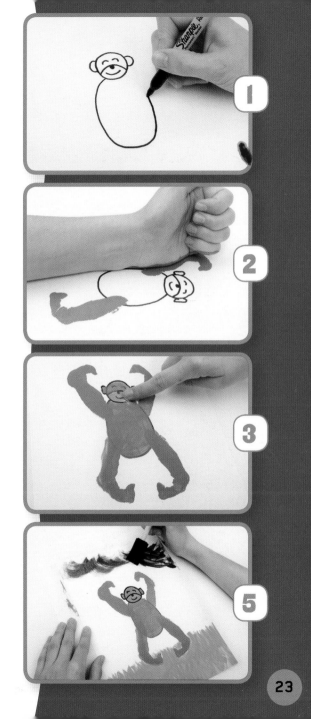

glossary

background – the area behind the main person or thing in a picture.

crack – to break open.

drawer – a sliding box that can be pulled out of a piece of furniture.

hind – located in the back or rear.

insect – a small creature with two or four wings, six legs, and a body with three sections.

intelligent – having the ability to acquire and use knowledge.

knuckle – one of the places where a finger or thumb bends.

noisy – making loud noises.

palm – the inside of your hand between your wrist and fingers.

primate – a mammal with developed hands and feet, a large brain, and a short nose, such as a human, ape, or monkey.

repel – to make something go away.